PLACES TO VISIT IN WASHINGTON DC

Geography Grade 1
Children's Explore the World Books

BABY PROFESSOR
EDUCATION KIDS

Speedy Publishing LLC
40 E. Main St. #1156
Newark, DE 19711
www.speedypublishing.com
Copyright 2017

All Rights reserved. No part of this book may be reproduced or used in any way or form or by any means whether electronic or mechanical, this means that you cannot record or photocopy any material ideas or tips that are provided in this book

There are many buildings, monuments, memorials and museums to visit when you travel to our Nation's Capital, Washington, D.C.

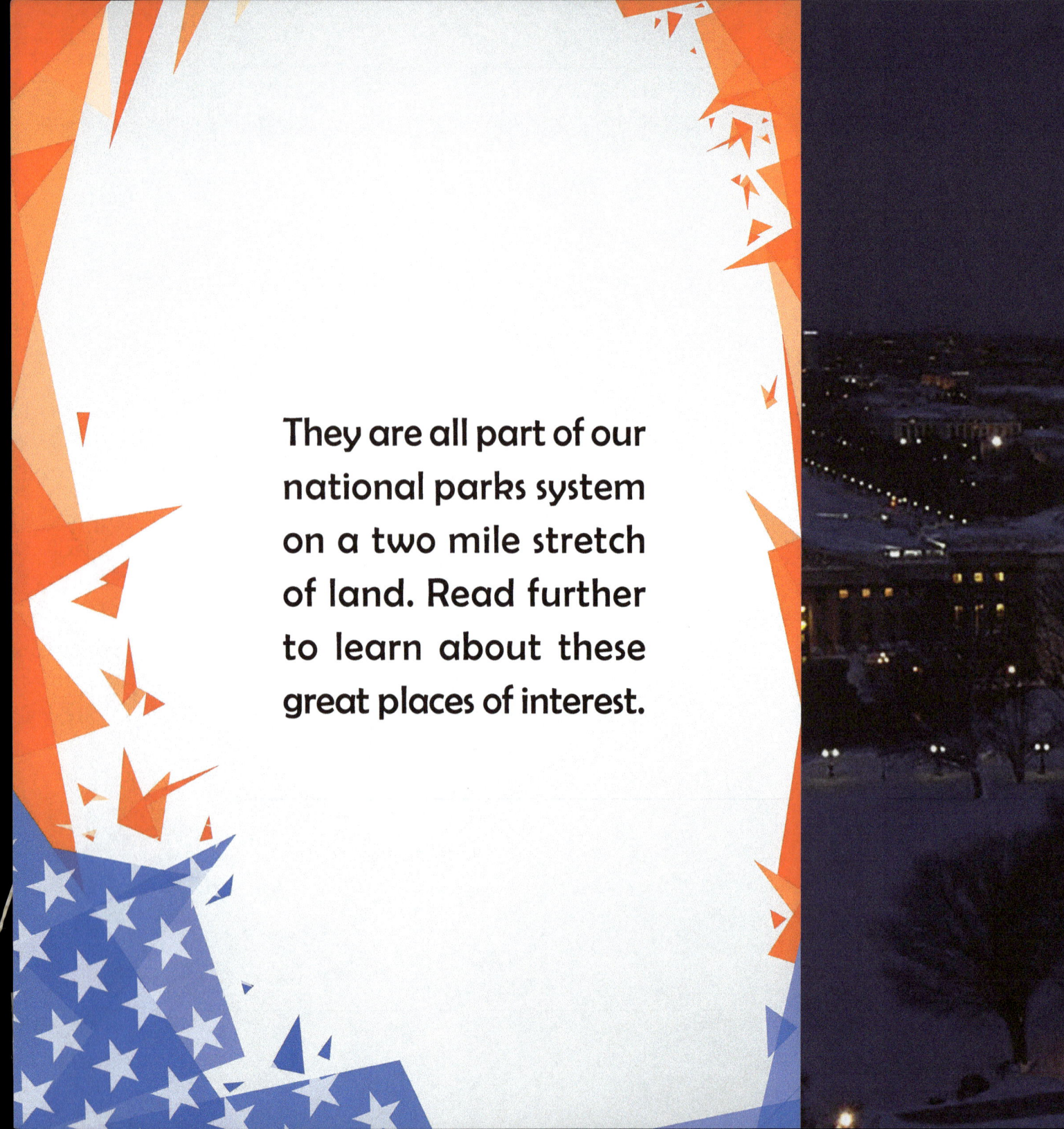

They are all part of our national parks system on a two mile stretch of land. Read further to learn about these great places of interest.

National Mall

THE NATIONAL MALL

The National Mall is in downtown Washington, D.C. and is comprised of many government buildings, museums and famous memorials. It includes a two mile stretch of land from the Lincoln Memorial to the Capitol Building. Be sure to bring your comfortable walking shoes or sneakers!

THE UNITED STATES CAPITOL

This is one of the most important buildings and its architecture is impressive. For two centuries, it has housed the meeting chambers for the Senate and the House of Representatives. Started in 1793, it has been through several phases of construction and today stands as the monument to the people of America and their government.

United States Capitol

Washington Monument

THE WASHINGTON MONUMENT

The Washington Monument is the center of the Mall and is a towering memorial to President George Washington. You can purchase tickets and take the elevator to the top for a gorgeous 360-degree view of our nation's Capital.

WORLD WAR II MEMORIAL

This is a new, beautiful memorial, which stands directly in front of a reflecting pool. It consists of 56 pillars and two small triumphal arches between the Washington Monument and the Lincoln Memorial. On May 29, 2004, it was dedicated by President George W. Bush, after opening in April of 2004.

World War II Memorial

Lincoln Memorial

THE LINCOLN MEMORIAL

This Memorial is in honor of our 16th President, Abraham Lincoln. It can be found at the west end of the Mall, across from the Washington Monument.

THE JEFFERSON MEMORIAL

This is the memorial of President Thomas Jefferson, who authored the Declaration of Independence. It is situated at the southwest are of the mall.

Jefferson Memorial

The White House

The White House is not part of the mall, but is located north of the Washington Monument, where you can catch a glimpse of this famous residence.

THE SMITHSONIAN AIR AND SPACE MUSEUM

The Smithsonian Air and Space Museum is located at the southeast corner of the Mall, next to the Museum of the American Indian, across from the National Gallery, and fairly close to the Capitol building. You will see historical items, including but not limited to, the Spirit of St. Louis as well as the first plane flown by the Wright Brothers. You will also be able to touch a moon rock.
That is truly something to remember.

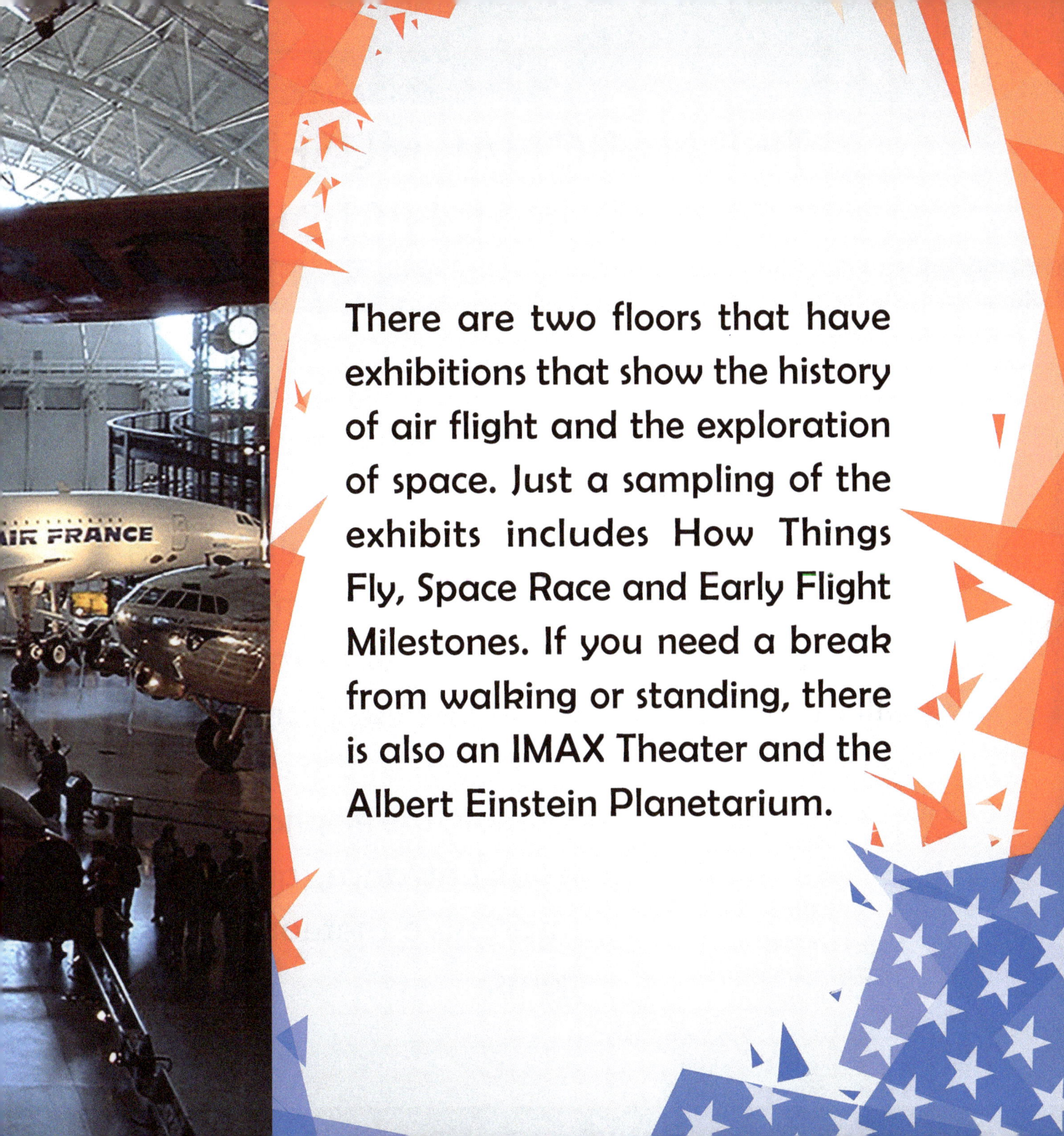

There are two floors that have exhibitions that show the history of air flight and the exploration of space. Just a sampling of the exhibits includes How Things Fly, Space Race and Early Flight Milestones. If you need a break from walking or standing, there is also an IMAX Theater and the Albert Einstein Planetarium.

THE NATIONAL MUSEUM OF NATURAL HISTORY

This museum is known to be visited more than any other Smithsonian Museum. It is a great place for the entire family to have fun, learn and explore. It is located on the Mall not too far from the Washington Monument. If you decide to look at and read every exhibit, you will be here for quite a while, but you can also just take in the highlights such as the dinosaurs, animals, the elephant in the front entrance, and some impressive meteorites and gems.

National Museum of Natural History

Some of the more popular exhibits include Dinosaur Hall, Mammal Hall, the Hall of Geology, Gems, and Minerals, the Insect Zoo, the Ocean Zoo, the Butterfly Pavilion and the Fossil Lab. There is also an IMAX theatre where you can sit back and watch a movie.

MUSEUM OF AMERICAN HISTORY

At this museum, you will see great pieces right out of the history books. You will find a little bit of everything here, from Richard Petty's race car, back to the Star-Spangled Banner flag. While there are many historical artifacts, there are also sports, movie, pop music and others.

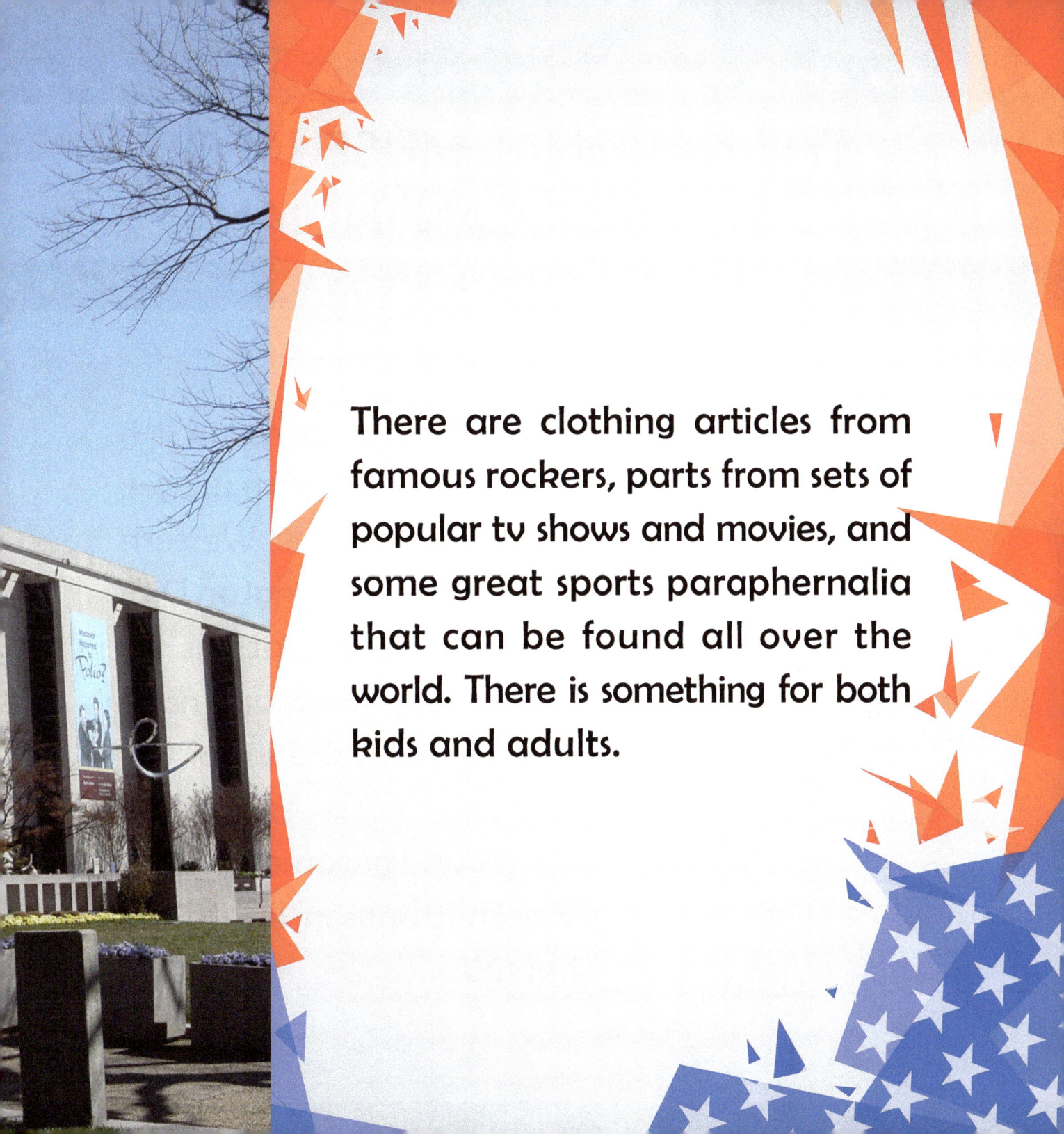

There are clothing articles from famous rockers, parts from sets of popular tv shows and movies, and some great sports paraphernalia that can be found all over the world. There is something for both kids and adults.

THE NATIONAL MUSEUM OF THE AMERICAN INDIAN

This museum is part of the Smithsonian and it is dedicated to the history, life, literature, languages, and arts of Native Americans in the Western Hemisphere. The one located in Washington D.C. is only one of three locations. Foundations for its present collections were assembled originally in New York City at the former Museum of the American Indian, established in 1916, and became a part of the Smithsonian Institution in 1990.

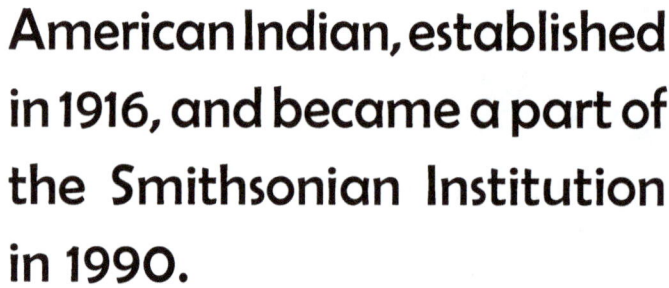

Museum of the American Indian

THE BEST WAYS TO GET AROUND THE MALL

Walking is one of the best ways to see the Mall, if you are in good health and enjoy exercise. However, there is a lot of walking, particularly if you are planning to walk it and view the memorials and museums. It will probably take at least two days and you will want to take a break every so often. Keep in mind that the distance is two miles from the Lincoln Memorial to the Capitol building.

Tour buses are also available to take you from one memorial to another one and are not very expensive if walking is not your thing

Bicycles are available for rent which can be enjoyable for everyone in the family.

Segway Tours are also available, but you have to be at least 16 years old in order to ride on one.

Segway tour

FOOD AT THE MALL

There are not too many restaurants located at the National Mall. Several of the Smithsonian Museums do have restaurants. There is a McDonalds at the Air and Space Museum which might work as a quick lunch. You can also bring a picnic lunch and use it as an opportunity to rest.

OTHER PLACES TO VISIT AROUND D.C.

Smithsonian National Zoological Park

THE SMITHSONIAN NATIONAL ZOO

Some of the favorite exhibits include the Giant Pandas Habitat, Elephant Trails, the Great Ape House, the Great Cats Exhibit, the Reptile Discovery Center, and a Kid's Farm where kids learn how farmers take care of farm animals such as alpacas, cows, rabbits, hogs, and lots more. The National Zoo is located approximately 3.5 miles north of Washington, D.C.

Bureau Of Engraving And Printing

THE BUREAU OF ENGRAVING AND PRINTING

Here you will learn how paper money is created. The tour will walk you through each step from the special paper that is used, the ink, and the process of printing. You will enjoy observing the big stacks of money that are real as it is getting printed right before your eyes. This tour takes about 30 minutes and is quite enjoyable. It is located not too far from the National Mall.

THE IWO JIMA MEMORIAL

Only a short distance from downtown D.C., this Marine Corps Memorial is an impressive and beautiful statue that honors the great women and men that fought for our freedom.

The Marine Corps War Memorial

The inspiration for this Memorial came from 1945 photograph of the six Marines raising a United States flag at the top of Mount Suribachi during World War II at the Battle of Iwo Jima, taken by Joe Rosenthal, an Associated Press combat photographer. The memorial was designed by sculptor Felix de Weldon and Horace W. Peaslee, an architect.

THE OLD POST OFFICE TOWER

This is a part of the National Parks Services and is a great place to get some great views of the D.C. area. It was finished in 1899. It was the city's main post office until the year 1914. After that, its primary function was an office building. During the 1920s it was almost demolished during construction of the complex known as the Federal Triangle.

Old Post Office and Clock Tower

Federal Triangle

Again, in the 1970s it was almost torn down for completion of the Federal Triangle. In 1976 and 1983, major renovations took place. A food court was added during the 1983 renovation as well as retail space. In 2013 the property was leased to Donald Trump, through one of his holding companies "DJT Holdings LLC". Trump then developed it into a luxurious hotel named the Trump International Hotel Washington, D.C., which then opened in 2016.

THE NATIONAL ARCHIVES

It won't take you long to walk through and see some of our most precious documents including the Constitution, the Bill of Rights, and the Declaration of Independence.

National Archives Building

DISCOVERY THEATER

The Discovery Theater is part of the Smithsonian and puts shows on for younger audiences. These shows take place at different locations so you will want to check their schedules.

There is so much history to learn and see, you won't want to miss anything. You may even want to make a second trip to see something that you may have missed the first time. For additional information on things to see in Washington, D.C., you can go to your local library, research the internet, and ask questions of your teachers, family and friends.

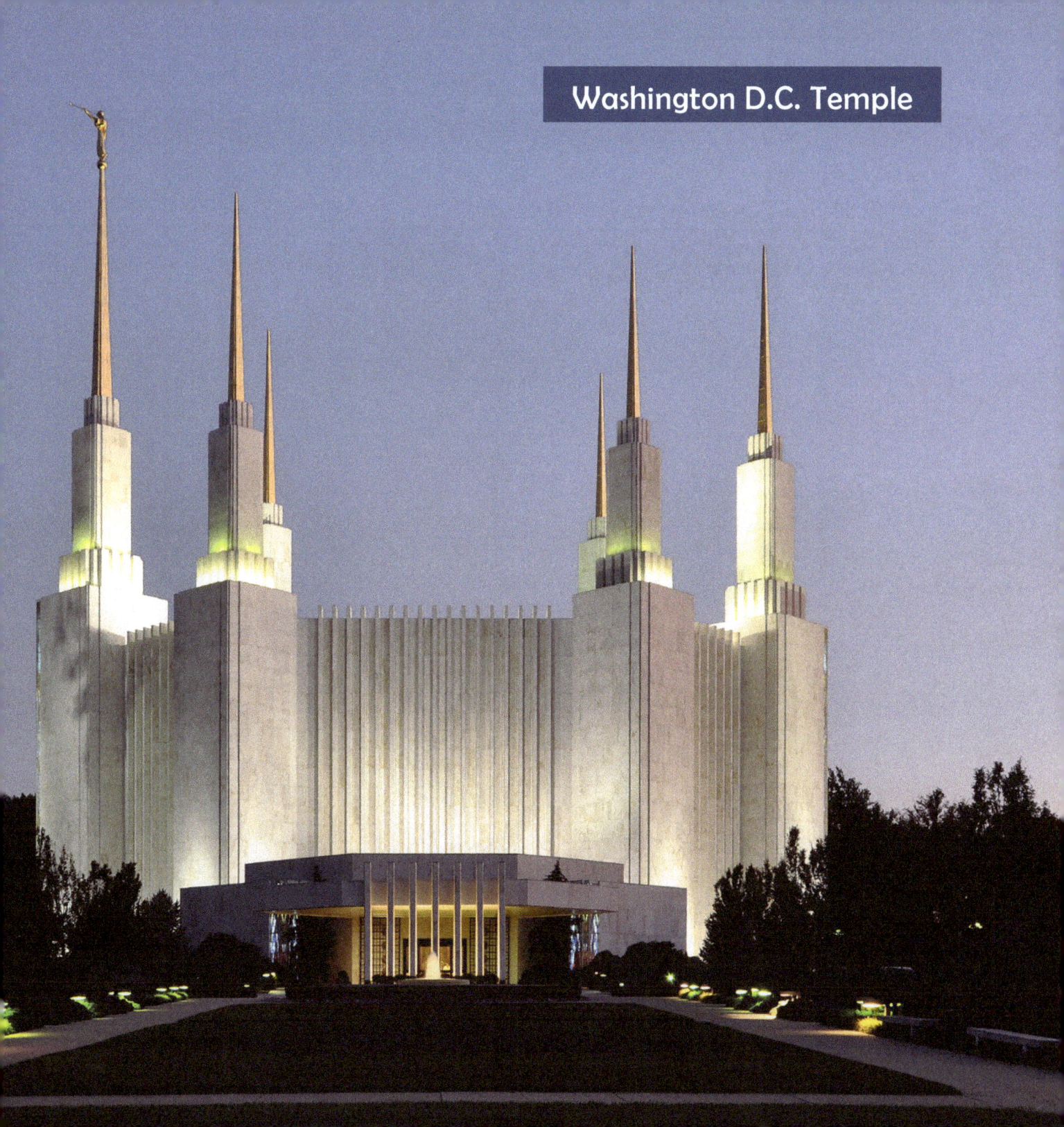
Washington D.C. Temple

Visit

BABY PROFESSOR
EDUCATION KIDS

www.BabyProfessorBooks.com

to download Free Baby Professor eBooks and view our catalog of new and exciting Children's Books

CPSIA information can be obtained
at www.ICGtesting.com
Printed in the USA
BVHW012255130222
628923BV00022BA/411